M10 and M36 Tank Destroyers 1942–53

S J Zaloga · Illustrated by P Sarson & M Badrocke

First published in Great Britain in 2002 by Osprey Publishing,
Midland House, West Way, Botley, Oxford OX2 0PH, UK
443 Park Avenue South, New York, NY 10016, USA
Email: info@ospreypublishing.com

CIP Data for this publication is available from the British Library
ISBN 1 84176 469 8

Editor: Simone Drinkwater
Design: Melissa Orrom Swan
Index by Alison Worthington
Originated by Magnet Harlequin, Uxbridge, UK
Printed in China through World Print Ltd.

05 06 07 08 10 9 8 7 6 5 4 3

For a catalogue of all books published by Osprey Military
and Aviation please contact:

NORTH AMERICA
Osprey Direct, 2427 Bond Street, University Park, IL 60466, USA
E-mail: info@ospreydirectusa.com

ALL OTHER REGIONS
Osprey Direct UK, P.O. Box 140, Wellingborough,
Northants, NN8 2FA, UK
E-mail: info@ospreydirect.co.uk

www.ospreypublishing.com

Author's note

The author is indebted for the help of many people who assisted on this project
and would like to thank Joe DeMarco, Jeff McKaughan, Peter Brown and Mark
Hayward who provided archival material from their own research. Thanks also
to Charles Lemons and Candace Fuller of the Patton Museum at Ft. Knox,
Kentucky, for their help with access to their superb archive and to their restored
M10 3-inch GMC. Thanks also go to the staff of the library, archive and special
collection branch of the US Army Military History Institute (MHI) at the US Army
War College, Carlisle Barracks, Pennsylvania, and the staff of the US National
Archives and Records Administration (NARA).

Over the years, a number of dubious names have been associated with the
M10 and M36 tank destroyers. The M10 is sometimes referred to as the
Wolverine, an unofficial nickname sometimes used in wartime Chrysler
advertising. It was never used by the US Army. The British M10C 17-pdr. was
referred to in at least one post-war report as Achilles, but this name was never
widely used by British forces. The M36 is sometimes referred to as the
Jackson, but this appears to be an entirely specious, postwar invention. None
of these names are used in this account in order to avoid perpetuating these
misnomers.

Artist's note

M10 AND M36 TANK DESTROYERS 1942-53

INTRODUCTION

While many armies used tank destroyers during World War II, the US Army gave them a far more central role in its mechanized doctrine. The M10 3-inch gun motor carriage was the most significant of these, and served from the first battles in Tunisia in 1943 to the end of the war. It was not the first choice of tank destroyer advocates, but it proved to be a versatile and dependable design. By 1944, its time had passed as increasing numbers of heavily armored Panthers and Tigers appeared on the battlefield. A version with a more powerful 90mm gun, the M36, was quickly pushed into service and became the principal type during the fighting in Germany in 1945. Both types quickly disappeared from US service after the war, but the M36 was exported in significant numbers throughout the 1950s. It saw service in many regional conflicts, even as late as the 1990s in Yugoslavia.

A dramatic view of three M10 tank destroyers advancing through Mönchen-Gladbach on March 1 1945, when the town was captured by the 29th Division during Operation Grenade. Although the M10 was not favored by the Tank Destroyer Command which viewed it as a hasty expedient, it proved to be more versatile and useful than the flawed tank destroyer doctrine on which it was based. (US Army)

TANK DESTROYER ORIGINS

The defeat of France in June 1940 shocked the US Army and started a major debate about future US force structure. It ended the squabbling over the role of the tank on the modern battlefield, and led to the formation of the Armored Force in July 1940. However, there was still some debate about how to best handle enemy tanks, and there was a strong lobby amongst artillery officers to assign anti-tank artillery for this mission. In May 1941, Gen. George C. Marshall, the army chief of staff, ordered that immediate action must be taken to deploy an offensive anti-tank weapon and organization to deal with the panzer threat. The US Army concluded that traditional anti-tank tactics relying on a thin cordon of anti-tank guns could be too easily breached by the concentration of panzers against a single point. In place of this tactic, the Army wanted to field an anti-tank weapon that could be held in reserve behind the battle line and then rapidly moved forward to staunch the flow of panzers once enemy intentions were clear. In the wake of a conference at the Army War College in July 1941, expedient anti-tank vehicles were ordered into development. These were strongly influenced by French accounts of anti-tank guns mounted on trucks and employed in the 1940 campaign. Two designs were quickly fielded to satisfy this requirement, the M6 37mm gun motor carriage (GMC) and the M3 75mm GMC. The M6 37mm GMC consisted of a standard Fargo three-quarter ton truck with a 37mm gun firing over the rear. The M3 75mm GMC consisted of an M3 half-track with a World War I vintage French 75mm gun firing over the front and was accepted for US Army use on 31 October 1941 in time for participation in the autumn wargames. Both were clap-trap affairs with serious technical and tactical problems. These two designs were regarded as a short-term solution until a custom-built anti-tank vehicle could be developed.

The M5 3-inch gun motor carriage was the first attempt to develop a self-propelled 3-inch anti-tank weapon. The army planned to acquire 1,580 of this clap-trap design in 1942, but the program was cancelled when the pilot vehicle broke down repeatedly in tests. (US Army)

RIGHT The pilot of the T35 3-inch gun motor carriage consisted of an M4A2 medium tank with a new open-top cast turret with a three-inch gun. This design was short-lived, as the Philippines campaign suggested that more attention should be paid to angling armor plate to improve its protective features. (US Army)

The head of the general staff planning branch for the tank destroyers, Lt.Col. Andrew Bruce, characterized the ideal tank destroyer as a fast cruiser rather than a battleship like contemporary tanks. His idea was for a vehicle faster than a tank with a more powerful gun but less armor than a tank. The senior commander of Army Ground Forces (AGF), Gen. Lesley McNair, was an artilleryman and strongly opposed the use of a

ABOVE **Another short-lived tank destroyer was the M9 3-inch GMC which mated a 3-inch anti-aircraft gun to a modified M3 medium tank chassis. Although more durable than the tinker-toy M5 tank destroyer, the M9 was a mediocre design that suffered a well-warranted cancellation when it was realized that there were only enough guns available to build about two dozen of the vehicles. (US Army)**

"$35,000 medium tank to destroy another tank when the job can be done by a gun costing a fraction as much." New anti-tank battalions were formed in the fall of 1941, and deployed in the Louisiana and Carolina maneuvers. The name of the units was changed to "tank destroyers" as it was felt that the old name suggested traditional passive defensive tactics. After further debate, a Tank Destroyer Tactical and Firing Center was organized under Col. Bruce in November 1941. Plans were laid to form 53 tank destroyer battalions, all under centralized general headquarters command. Of the 44 battalions formed on December 15 1941, 16 were heavy battalions to be equipped with 24 self-propelled 3-inch guns and 12 self-propelled 37mm guns, while the remainder were towed and self-propelled light battalions, armed with the 37mm gun. With the outbreak of war in December 1941, these efforts took on a new urgency. On April 23 1942, the Army decided to standardize on a single type of tank destroyer battalion using the heavy configuration, so putting more pressure on Ordnance to complete a satisfactory 3-inch GMC design. The Tank Destroyer Board began to examine some 200 different design proposals for its 3-inch gun tank destroyer.

The first of these to receive serious attention was a 1940 Cleveland Tractor Co. (Cletrac) proposal which mounted a 3-inch T9 anti-aircraft gun on its MG2 airfield towing tractor. The project was formally approved in January 1941 as the T1 3-inch GMC and a pilot was delivered in November 1941 for trials. Ordnance was not entirely happy

about the choice of chassis, and in October 1941, an alternative design was approved for development, the 3-inch GMC T24 which mounted the 3-inch M1918 anti-aircraft gun on an M3 medium tank chassis. The conversion was quite simple, and a pilot was delivered in November 1941.

Neither design was entirely satisfactory and both were sent back for redesign. Due to the urgent need for tank destroyers, the Adjutant General approved standardization of the T1 3-inch GMC in January 1941 as the M5, and authorized immediate procurement of 1,580 vehicles subject to the approval of the Tank Destroyer Center. By this time, the Army had concluded that the T24 design had been too hasty resulting in a vehicle with an excessive silhouette. As a result, on December 31 1941, Ordnance began work on a similar design with a lower silhouette, the 3-inch GMC T40. As in the case of the T1, wartime pressures led to its premature adoption as the substitute standard 3-inch GMC M9 in May 1942.

While final design of these two tank destroyers was underway, a number of army officials began to

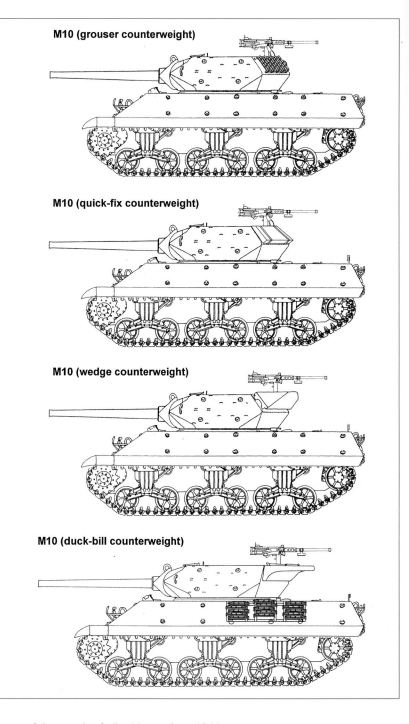

M10 (grouser counterweight)

M10 (quick-fix counterweight)

M10 (wedge counterweight)

M10 (duck-bill counterweight)

Scale line drawings of a number of M10 variants. (Author)

criticize the vehicles as too hasty and improvised. In November 1941, Ordnance recommended the design of a turreted tank destroyer using the new 3-inch gun from the M6 heavy tank mounted on an M4A2 medium tank chassis. The original conception was to mount the gun in a partial turret with armor protecting only the front quadrant. When finally approved for development as the 3-inch GMC T35, the design had changed to an open-topped turret with all-around protection. As detail design continued, Ordnance began to receive reports from US troops

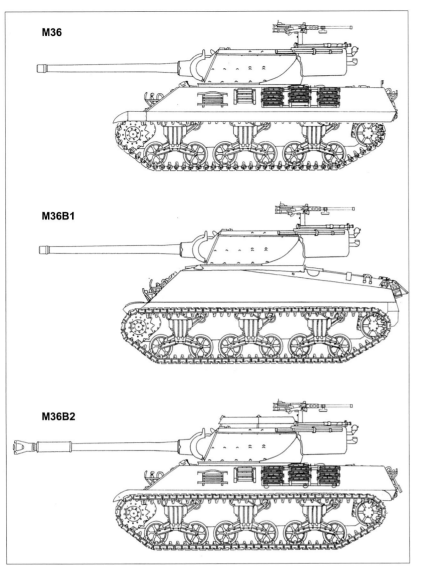

M36

M36B1

M36B2

Scale line drawings of various
M36 vehicles. (Author)

involved in the fighting in the Philippines in December 1941–January 1942. The armored units were very critical of pre-war designs using vertical armor which proved too easy to penetrate. This led to immediate interest in adopting sloped armor on future designs with an aim to increase the effective thickness of armor plate against enemy anti-tank guns. As a result, a second configuration of the T35 entered development, the T35E1, which had a new hull design with sloped sides. Pilots of both types were delivered by General Motors' Fisher Body Division to Aberdeen Proving Ground in April 1942. Following a demonstration of both designs, on May 2 1942, the Army decided in favor of the T35E1 configuration. The pilots used a common cast turret, but the Army preferred a welded design for the production vehicle. The pilots were considered to be too heavy at 30.5 tons, and to reduce this to 29 tons, the hull armor was reduced from one inch on the hull to three-quarters of an inch, with decreases on the other surfaces as well. This caused some concern at the Proving Ground, which recommended that bosses be welded to the sides to permit attachment of appliqué armor panels at a later date if needed. In the event, the appliqué armor panels were never manufactured. In June 1942, Ordnance recommended the modified T35E1 for standardization as the 3-inch GMC M10.

As the M10 design reached maturity, the Army began to have second thoughts about the M5 and M9 3-inch tank destroyers. The M9 tank destroyer program was the first to be cancelled on August 20 1942, when it was determined that there were only 28 guns available for the conversion. The M5 proved to be an embarrassment during trials as it had grown considerably in weight since its original design. During May 1942 tests at Ft. Bragg, it broke its track twice and caught fire, prematurely ending the trials. After repairs it was given a top speed test and cross-country test at Aberdeen Proving Ground during which it became so damaged that comparative trials against the M10 proved impossible. The plan to manufacture the M5 was cancelled on September 30 1942. With its two competitors eliminated, the M10 remained the only 3-inch gun tank destroyer deemed suitable for army use in the late summer of 1942. The Army was so desperate for tank destroyers that the M10 was given the AA1 priority production rating, higher than the M4 medium tank program at the time. Since there was some concern that M4A2 chassis production would not be adequate, a second version, the M10A1, was also approved for production. This was essentially the same as the M10 except based on the M4A3 tank chassis with the Ford gasoline engine instead of the twin GM diesels of the M4A2 chassis.

INITIAL PRODUCTION

Most of the final development work on the M10 concentrated on the new turret design. A novel trunnion design was selected to make it easier to remove the gun assembly in the field. This also made it possible to later mount alternative weapons in the turret including the 105mm howitzer or the British 17-pdr. gun. The original welded turret design was hexagonal, but the production design was pentagonal. Initial mock-ups had periscopes for the turret crew in the front roof, but on the production turret, the roof was reduced in depth and the periscopes eliminated. Production of the M10 started at the Fisher Tank Arsenal at Grand Blanc, Michigan, in September and 105 vehicles were finished by the end of the month. The M10 cost $47,900, compared to $60,200 for the comparable M4A2 tank, a price difference of about 25 percent.

The first M10s were immediately dispatched to tank destroyer battalions at training facilities in the United States including the 636th TD Battalion at Camp Edwards and the 703rd TD Battalion at Camp Pickett. The M10A1 entered production a month later at Ford Motor Company with the first three being manufactured in October 1942. Once the M10A1 entered service, the practice began of equipping battalions with one type or another, not both. So of the six battalions equipped in December 1942, the 704th, 705th and 706th all received M10A1, while the 629th, 809th and 893rd all received M10 tank destroyers.

In the haste to push the M10 into production, a number of flaws in the design went unappreciated. One of the most serious problems was the imbalance in the turret caused by the heavy gun barrel. This was not serious when the vehicle was on level ground, but on a slope greater than 4 degrees it made it difficult or impossible for the crew to traverse the turret. This problem had actually been

This is the first series production M10 3-inch gun motor carriage, completed in September 1942. The problem of turret imbalance plagued the early production series, and the first attempt to rectify the problem was to stow the track grousers on the upper rear turret plate as seen here. This did not prove adequate, even when the .50 cal. heavy machine gun was also added to the rear. (US Army)

The next attempt to correct the turret problem was to adopt a set of "quick-fix" counterweights to the rear of the turret as seen here on an M10 in Oran, Morocco, in 1943. This particular vehicle is fitted with the lead counterweights that can be distinguished by the pair of extra steel straps holding them in place. In contrast, steel and cast iron versions were supposed to be bolted in place. With the grousers removed from the turret rear, another grouser rack was fitted to the hull side, though here it is seen carrying a few track blocks and not grousers. Another early change evident here is the stirrup gun rest on the upper rear plate for use when the vehicle was traveling to lock the gun in position. (US Army)

noticed earlier, but the Tank Destroyer Center was reluctant to add turret counterweights to the rear of the turret since the vehicle was already three tons over its design specifications. The initial solution was to shift the grouser stowage to the upper rear panels of the turret, and to mount the .50 cal. machine gun on the turret rear. These changes were retrofitted on early series production vehicles, but were not sufficient to solve the imbalance. As the first vehicles began to be issued in the fall of 1942, complaints increased. There was general agreement that a rear counter-balance would be needed as soon as possible. Ordnance wanted the counter-balances to be sufficient to allow the turret to be easily traversed even when on a 15 degree slope.

The pace of deployment of M10 tank destroyers was so rapid that it was decided to approach the problem in a two phase manner: a "quick-fix" counterweight, and a production counterweight. A quick-fix counterweight was developed which was simple enough that it could be fabricated by battalion maintenance shops for units already equipped with the M10. The design was completed on December 21 1942, and its mild steel version weighed 2,400 pounds. To make it easier for local fabrication, three alternative designs were prepared using steel, cast iron, or lead. All three were externally identical except for the lead version which was not as thick, and which had a pair of steel bands strapped on each counterweight for added strength. Some tank destroyer units, notably those at 636th Tank Destroyer Bn. at Camp Edwards, had already begun local experiments with counterweights, some weighing over 7,000 pounds.

Units destined for overseas deployment were authorized to add their own counterweights based on a January 16 1943 provisional work order, while other units and depots waited for a supply of counterweights from the Fisher plant. The quick-fix counterweights, designated E7790 (right side) and E7791 (left side), were designed to employ portions of the

existing grouser rack, reinforced by bolting the weights to the upper rear turret panels. Fisher shipped the first factory-produced counterweights to depots on 7 January 1943, and a production order for 284 kits was issued in early February 1943.

By early January, Fisher had completed the design of a new wedge-shaped heavy 3,700 pound cast-iron design designated E7992 and E7993. The quick-fix design did not prove adequate to allow the turret to be easily traversed on slopes of 12 degrees, while the heavy design proved to be more effective. All turrets manufactured after 5 January were drilled for attachment of the new wedge production counterweights which were added to vehicles starting on 25 January 1943. Tests of the production type at Camp Edwards proved satisfactory and this became the standard production configuration of the M10 until June 1943. About 650 M10 and M10A1 tank destroyers were manufactured in the initial configuration without the turret counterweight, and about 2,850 with the heavy wedge counterweight.

Even though the new production counterweight significantly improved the problem, it was still far from ideal, being too heavy. As a result, a third counterweight design was undertaken at Fisher and was ready for tests in late March 1943. This cast steel design reduced the weight to 2,500 pounds and was soon dubbed the "duck-bill" counterweight due to its shape. Officially, the parts were designated as the E8010 and E8011. This design was made more efficient by reconfiguring the rear upper walls of the M10 turret to a near vertical position, and extending the counterweight much further back from the center-point of the turret.

Two other alternatives were considered to counterweights. By installing an Oilgear traversing motor in the turret as used on the M4 medium tank, the problem would be solved since the motor could

The turret imbalance was better solved by the addition of this pair of wedge-shaped heavy counterweights, introduced into series production in January 1943. This particular M10, nicknamed "Pistol Packin' Mama", served with the Tank Destroyer School at Camp Hood, Texas, in October 1943, and carries the force's emblem, the black panther, painted under the rear of the turret. (US Army)

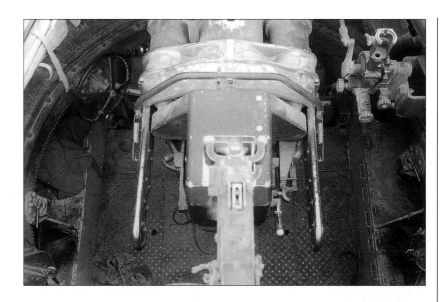

ABOVE **A view inside the turret of the M10 shows the gun breech of the vehicle, partially obscured by the .50 cal. heavy machine gun. The gunner sat in the left forward side of the turret, with the loader behind him. The commander sat in the right side, and an additional seat was provided for the co-driver who acted as an assistant to the loader if necessary. (US Army)**

traverse the turret even without the counterweights. A single M10 was modified with the Oilgear device, but was not tested until late September 1943. Although this had many advantages, by the time the test was completed M10 production was nearly complete so no action was taken. A second proposal was to move the gun back further into the turret, reducing the overhang of the barrel which was the source of the problem. However, this required a substantial redesign of the turret and it was quickly determined that it would interfere with elevating and loading the gun.

With no other solution on hand, in June 1943 it was decided to shift to the production of the enlarged turret with the duck-bill counterweights. This configuration entered production in late June 1943 as components for the earlier turret configuration became exhausted. About 3,200 M10 and M10A1 were completed with the duck-bill counterweight. There was no changes in the designation of the M10 or M10A1 whether fitted with no counterweight, the quick-fix counterweight, the heavy counterweight, or the final duck-bill counterweight with the enlarged turret.

While the counterweight changes were the most noticeable modification to the original M10 design, there were many other smaller changes. The location of the turret traverse hand-wheel was too far back, interfering with its proper use, and so it was moved forward. A second turret lock was added as it was found that the turret could move dangerously during travel. A turret travel lock was also added on the turret roof to prevent the gun from moving during transit. The initial configuration of the driver and co-driver's seat proved flawed and had to be redesigned. A "stirrup" gun rest was added on the rear deck to prevent the gun from moving during transit. These features were added on production vehicles by late December 1942, and vehicles already deployed were modified by unit workshops starting in January 1943. Since the grousers had been removed from the turret by the new counterweights, in March 1943, it was decided to move them to the hull sides on brackets attached to the protruding bosses. This change was introduced on vehicles starting in early April 1943.

The original production batches of M10 and M10A1 had fire controls limited to a direct fire telescope. Given the influence of artillery officers in the Tank Destroyer Command, there was some interest in providing it with indirect fire capability as well. After various configuration were tested, Ordnance finally settled on the use of an azimuth indicator and a gunner's quadrant. This configuration was approved in May 1943 and went into production shortly after. Some vehicles already manufactured were later upgraded with this feature in the field. In July 1943, the side bosses for attaching appliqué armor were left off since the intended up-armor kit was never manufactured.

Even the heavy wedge counterweight was not entirely successful, leading to the final enlarged turret with the "duck-bill" counterweight in June 1943. On this version, the turret rear panel was extended backward, providing more interior space. This particular vehicle is an M10A1, built on the M4A3 medium tank chassis. It is very difficult to distinguish the M10 from the M10A1 except for the fuel filler caps on the engine deck, and the exhaust deflectors on the hull rear, not evident in this view. All M10A1 tank destroyers were kept in the United States for training, and most were later converted into M36 90mm gun motor carriages. (US Army)

M10 PRODUCTION

	M10	M10A1
Sep 42	105	0
Oct 42	170	3
Nov 42	137	18
Dec 42	199	7
Jan 43	276	56
Feb 43	340	116
Mar 43	330	150
Apr 43	428	133
May 43	416	123
Jun 43	400	133
Jul 43	402	124
Aug 43	465	131
Sep 43	498	49
Oct 43	350	150
Nov 43	237	220
Dec 43	240	0
Jan 44	0	300*
Total	**4,993**	**1,713**

*without turrets

INTO SERVICE

The Tank Destroyer Command was unhappy with the M10 design almost from the outset. During the May 1942 demonstration of the T35 pilots at Aberdeen, the head of the Tank Destroyer Command, Gen. Andrew

Bruce, was unwilling to approve standardization of the design, feeling it was just another expedient like the M3 75mm GMC that preceded it. Due to the tank destroyer doctrine that stressed aggressive tactics, Bruce wanted a vehicle that was markedly faster than contemporary tanks, and was pinning his hopes on the new T70 design, which would emerge late in 1943 as the M18 76mm GMC. The Army went ahead with development and production anyway. Gen. W. B. Palmer, who headed the Special Armored Vehicle Board to look at army requirements, later complained to Bruce that he was never satisfied with any Ordnance proposals and had to be more realistic about what type of vehicle could actually be fielded in time to participate in the upcoming campaigns. The Tank Destroyer Board, now located at the new facilities at Camp Hood, Texas, put the M10 through its service trials in late 1942. In December 1942, the board concluded that the M10 was superior to any other tank destroyer available. However, the board was not happy with the M10 compared to the original requirement for a highly mobile 3-inch gun, since it had only a modest speed advantage over medium tanks, and only marginally better firepower. The Armored Force was no more happy with the design and in January 1943 concluded that it should be considered unsuitable for service since it was too close in performance to the existing M4 tank while having inadequate armor for tactical employment, an unbalanced turret, and poor traversing equipment.

The Army decided to limit overseas deployments to the diesel-powered M10 and to retain the gasoline-powered M10A1 in the United States for training. This was due to the higher production rate of the M10. When the M10 and M10A1 were finally tested side-by-side by the Tank Destroyer Board in September 1943, the board concluded that the M10A1 was automotively superior, in part due to the fact that the Ford engine weighed only 1,470 pounds compared to the 4,855 pounds of the twin diesels in the M10. However, by the time the test results were released in February 1944, the Army was already committed to using the M10 overseas in the combat zones, and most battalions were already deployed. The Tank Destroyer Command made the best of it, claiming that the diesel engines were less fire-prone in combat, when in fact ammunition fires were by far the most common source of catastrophic vehicle fires in combat.

The first commitment of tank destroyer battalions to combat took place during the North African campaign. Three battalions, the 601st, 701st and 805th, were deployed in Tunisia during

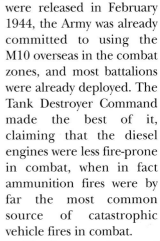

A number of other improvements to the M10 design were contemplated but not put into production. This pilot served as the test-bed for two new features. An armored enclosure was fitted over the engine access doors in the rear for unprepared river crossing and to make it easier to prepare for deep fording during amphibious operations. This pilot also has a modified turret with a bulge in the right turret panel to permit full traverse for the .50 cal. anti-aircraft machine gun. (US Army)

the January 1943 fighting. These were all equipped with the expedient M3 75mm GMC and M6 37mm GMC. Following the debacle at Kasserine Pass in March 1943 three additional battalions were sent to North Africa, the 813th still equipped with the older types, and the 776th and 899th TD Battalions, equipped with the new M10 3-inch GMC. The first combat use of the M10 involved the 899th Tank Destroyer Battalion during the fighting around El Guettar on 23 March 1943.

The battalion supported the 601st TD Battalion during an attack by about fifty tanks of 10.Panzer Division. The attack was beaten off and about 30 German tanks destroyed. However, the 601st lost 20 of its 28 M3 75mm SPMs and the 899th lost seven M10 3-inch GMCs. The fighting at El Guettar in late March was the sole example of the tank destroyer battalions being used according to doctrine as a concentrated force to repulse a massed tank attack. The two M10 battalions saw little tank fighting in the later phase of the campaign as by this time the German forces had been reduced in strength and seldom used panzers en masse. One of the M10 battalion commanders, Lt.Col. James Barney of the 776th TD Battalion, could not bear to see his 36 guns go to waste and so developed tactics and techniques for using the M10 as indirect fire artillery support when their anti-tank capabilities weren't needed. During the fighting in the approaches to Bizerte, the battalion shot up the German anti-tank defenses in the "Mousetrap" area, clearing the way for the final assault by the 1st Armored Division. As would be proven in the Italian campaign, artillery fire support would become one of the main missions of tank destroyers over the next year in the Mediterranean theater. Following the fighting in Tunisia, all of the tank destroyer battalions in North Africa were reequipped with M10 tank destroyers. Curiously enough, the battalions ended up with a hodge-podge of types with some units like the 894th TD Battalion receiving M10s with both the wedge-shaped counterweights and the latest duck-bill counterweights.

The employment of tank destroyers remained a serious bone of contention within the upper ranks of the US Army. Various factions saw the Tunisian campaign as vindicating their own point of view. The artillery branch, with the support of the head of Army Ground Forces, Gen. Lesley McNair, saw it as proving the value of towed anti-tank guns. McNair had already ordered the Tank Destroyer Center to begin to test a new towed 3-inch anti-tank gun in January 1943 and to develop battalion tactics for towed weapons. Maj. Gen. John Lucas, a special observer for the army chief of staff, concluded that "the Tank Destroyer has, in my opinion, failed to prove its usefulness...I believe that the

The M10 first went into combat service in North Africa in early 1943 with the 776th and 899th Tank Destroyer Battalions. They were early production types, fitted with the "quick-fix" counterweights as seen on this vehicle in Tunisia in March 1943. These units made use of field expedient camouflage, consisting of local mud daubed over the vehicle to lighten the dark olive drab color of the vehicles. (US Army)

The T72 76mm GMC was an attempt to solve the turret imbalance and weight problems by introducing the lighter 76mm gun developed for the M18 76mm tank destroyer. It was a pointless effort as Ordnance favored a 90mm gun, and the Tank Destroyer Command wanted the faster M18 tank destroyer. (US Army)

doctrine of an offensive weapon to 'slug it out' with the tank is unsound." Lucas supported the deployment of purely defensive anti-tank weapons such as anti-tank guns. Lt. Gen. Jacob Devers, who headed the Armored Force at the time, toured North Africa and concluded that "the separate tank destroyer arm is not a practical concept on the battle-field. Def-ensive anti-tank weapons are essentially artillery. Offensively, the best way to beat the tank is a better tank." All the commanders of II Corps in Tunisia including George Patton and Omar Bradley were unhappy with the performance of the offensively oriented tank destroyer doctrine, which proved unsuited to actual battlefield conditions. Due to McNair's influence on Army policy, in March 1943, fifteen tank destroyer battalions were converted from self-propelled to towed, a change that would prove to be a complete mistake. This renewed interest in towed anti-tank guns led to production of the M10 being halted at the end of 1943.

Fighting in Italy in 1943 and 1944 did little to settle the controversy. As many of the tank destroyer battalions in North Africa were in the process of converting to the M10, none took part in the campaign in Sicily except for the use of personnel for secondary assignments such as POW guards. Three of the newly equipped battalions were committed to the Salerno operation in September 1943, the 601st, 636th, and 645th TD Battalions. The battalions saw heavy fighting around the beach-head due to the presence of a significant amount of German armor. An M10, nicknamed "Jinx", commanded by Sgt. Edwin Yosts of the 636th TD Battalion became the first M10 ace of the war, knocking out five PzKpfw IV tanks during the September 14 1943 German counter-attack. Two further battalions arrived after the initial beach-head operations. As the Germans withdrew to the Volturno line, the tactics and missions of the tank destroyers changed. Encounters with panzers became extremely rare, and the four battalions in the theater were used increasingly for artillery fire support. By December 1943, the battalions were averaging 15,000 high explosive rounds per month and suffering from the unexpected problem of barrel wear. The 3-inch gun on the M10 had never been designed for the heavy volume of fire of a field artillery piece, and so the crews were obliged to learn the process for changing barrels with new tubes.

Tank fighting became more common after January 1944 when the Allies attempted to outflank the German Gustav line with an amphibious landing at Anzio. The 601st TD Battalion, attached to the 3rd Infantry Division, was used for direct fire support during the landing operation and soon encountered German PzKpfw IV tanks and StuG III assault guns. Four days later, the 894th TD Battalion was landed to support the British 1st Division. A third unit, the 645th TD Battalion, was landed prior to the major German counterattack on the landing zone later in the month. These units encountered some of the new heavy German armor for the first time during the fighting, including the Ferdinand assault gun, and the new Panther medium tank. During one of the most intense panzer attacks on February 29 1944, the M10s of the 601st TD Battalion were credited with knocking out 25 tanks and assault

guns. A fourth M10 unit, the 804th TD Battalion, arrived in March by which time the Anzio sector had turned into a costly stalemate. During the stalemate, the units began to tinker with improvements to the M10, including the addition of overhead armor to the exposed roofs of the M10. On May 11 1944, the Allies began a major offensive in Italy, breaking through the Gustav line at Cassino, and finally breaking out of the bridgehead at Anzio. Within weeks, they were in Rome. Following the capture of Rome, attention shifted to another theater, with the Allied landings at Normandy. Four tank destroyer battalions remained in Italy, but the remainder were assigned to take part in Operation Dragoon, the amphibious landings on the southern coast of France.

PRODUCTION CHANGES

A number of improvements to the M10 were considered during its production run. With the increasing number of amphibious landings and the need for elaborate wading kits, there was some interest in simplifying the process of preparing armored vehicles for amphibious operations. A project was initiated in January 1943 to create a well around the rear engine access panels to make the attachment of wading trunks quicker. A single M10 was modified in this fashion, though the project never proceeded any further since it also created access problems to the engine. The anti-aircraft machine gun position on the M10 was an after-thought, added in part to try to counter-balance the early turret. The machine gun could not be operated when the main gun was in use, since the gunner would be seriously injured by the recoiling gun. In addition, the traverse of the gun was limited to an arc about 125 degrees behind the vehicle due to its awkward location. There was some interest in improving the layout of this weapon, and so a single turret was

The narrow tracks of US tanks and tank destroyers proved ill-suited to the wet weather conditions in Europe in the fall of 1944 and winter of 1945. As an expedient, they were fitted with extended end-connectors for better floatation in mud. This sometimes caused problems on M10 and M36 tank destroyers as they could catch on the hull underhang. As a result, some units had ordnance depots cut off the underhang and remove the front fenders to prevent problems as is seen on this M36 operating in Cologne on March 3 1945, during the fight for the city. The .50 cal. heavy machine gun has been moved up to the left front corner of the turret and a .30 cal. machine gun added in its place above the turret bustle. (US Army)

modified with components from the M18 76mm GMC. This turret was placed on the same hull as was used for the deep wading trials, though there was no specific connection between the two study projects. In the event, neither was selected for incorporation into the M10 design.

By the end of 1943, 106 tank destroyer battalions had been formed. However, the demand for such units was on the decline due to their mixed performance in North Africa. A total of 61 battalions would eventually be deployed in the Mediterranean and European Theater of Operations (ETO), and 10 in the Pacific. The remaining 35 were broken up later for personnel or converted into other types of units. The declining number of battalions as well as the decision to begin converting units to towed anti-tank guns led to a severe decline in the requirements for M10 tank destroyers. As a result, the Army began to cut back on its production contracts. Production of the M10 at the Grand Blanc plant concluded in December 1943 after 4,993 had been completed. Ford's production of the M10A1 concluded in September 1944 after 1,038 had been built. However, assembly of the M10A1 was shifted to Grand Blanc and in October to November, a further 375 M10A1 were completed there. A final production batch of 300 M10A1 hulls were assembled at Grand Blanc in January 1944, but they were not fitted with turrets and were later converted into M36 tank destroyers. As a result, a total of 6,406 M10 and M10A1 were manufactured, not counting the final 300 hulls.

Another application for the surplus M10A1 was as a gun tractor. There was a need for an interim prime mover capable of towing the components of the very heavy 240mm howitzer and 120mm anti-aircraft gun until the delayed M6 high speed tractor became available. The Lima Tank Plant converted 209 M10A1 tank destroyers into the M35 prime mover from January to June 1944 by removing the turret and making a number of small changes on the hull. These were used by a number of heavy field artillery battalions including the 551st Field Artillery. One of the oddest conversions was the so-called "Sonic M10". This was part of a program to field a loudspeaker system that could be deployed near the front lines to broadcast realistic tank sounds to fool the enemy regarding the location of major US units. The M10 was selected for this deception scheme, and 24 were converted into "Special

The Army needed a heavy prime mover for the heavy 240mm howitzer and the 120mm anti-aircraft gun until the M6 high speed tractor became available. As a result, a small number of M35 prime movers were created by removing the turrets from M10A1 tank destroyers. This example is being used at the air defense school at Ft. Bliss, Texas, in 1944 towing a 120mm anti-aircraft gun. (US Army)

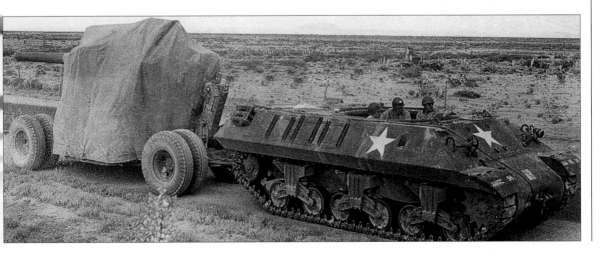

Cars" by deleting their main gun, and fitting a folding loudspeaker system into the turret well. They were first deployed with the 3132nd Signal Service Co. (Special) during the fighting on the outskirts of Brest, France, on August 23 1944, being used to mask the location of the planned assault. A second company, the 3133rd, was deployed to Italy where they were used during operations in the Sericho and Po valleys.

During the development of the rival M18 76mm GMC, Ordnance designed a new, lighter-weight 76mm gun better suited for use in tanks or tank destroyers. This gun fired the same projectile as the 3-inch gun, but was labeled as a 76mm gun since it used a different ammunition type with a new propellant casing that would not fit in the 3-inch gun. In view of the lingering problems with the heavy M7 3-inch gun, in March 1943 Ordnance authorized the construction of an M10 derivative, the T72 76mm GMC, as a possible substitute. Due to the lower weight of the gun and turret, the T72 weighed 2.2 tons less than the M10, and ammunition supply was increased by 45 rounds to 99 rounds. Two pilots were delivered in March and April 1943. However, the Tank Destroyer Command favored the deployment of the new M18 76mm GMC, and the program was cancelled in early 1944 due to a lack of interest.

Ordnance also began studies of more powerful guns for the tank destroyers, even though there was no user requirement. The potential use of the 90mm anti-aircraft gun was largely spurred on by reports of the German use of the 88mm anti-aircraft gun in the anti-tank role. The first serious attempt, the 90mm GMC T53, mated a 90mm antiaircraft gun to an M4 tank chassis. At an August 1942 conference, the Army Ground Forces and Ordnance agreed to begin producing 500 of these vehicles, with a further 3,500 contemplated. The Tank Destroyer command complained that the vehicle had not been adequately tested and that such a crude conversion was a step backward in tank destroyer design. In the event, the modified T53E1 proved such a poor design when tested that the production decision was later rescinded. Ordnance realized that for the 90mm gun to succeed, the weapon had to be redesigned into a smaller package to better fit into tanks and tank destroyers. In October 1942, Ordnance began

ABOVE **One of the oddest variants of the M10 was the so-called Sonic M10 of which two dozen were converted. The gun was removed and the barrel replaced with a dummy. An array of loudspeakers was mounted inside the turret, hinged so that they could be elevated for use as seen here, or folded inside when not in use. These were used in both France and Italy to deceive the Germans about the locations of US armored units by broadcasting fake armored vehicle sounds. (US Army)**

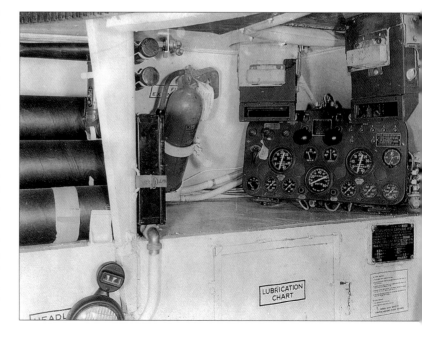

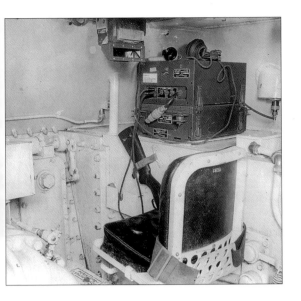

The co-driver in the M10 sat in the right side of the front hull and was responsible for operating the vehicle radio, usually the SCR-610 as seen here. (US Army)

work on developing an appropriate recoil and trunnion system for the proposed T7 90mm gun. One of the two pilot guns was mounted in an M10 late in 1942. Due to the original configuration of the turret trunnions to accept the 105mm howitzer or 17-pdr., the mounting proved straightforward. The 90mm T7 was not significantly heavier than the existing 3-inch gun, and as a result, the trials proceeded with little difficulty. Having been mounted in the first serial production M10 without turret counterweights, it had the usual problems of this type and the turret was deemed unsatisfactory for the 90mm gun. Due to the greater volume of the 90mm ammunition, it was quickly recognized that it would be better to develop a new turret that would cure the turret balance issue, add a power traverse, and increase the ammunition stowage. Gen. Bruce of the Tank Destroyer Command objected to the project, due to his disdain of the slow M10 chassis, the likelihood that the 90mm version would be even slower, and his belief that there was no need for a more powerful gun. He was ignored due to support from both the AGF and Ordnance, and the Tank Destroyer Command continued to be marginalized in army decisions on these issues due to its poor judgment in the past.

TANK DESTROYER GUN PERFORMANCE

Penetration in mm against armor at 30 degrees

	500 yards	1,000 yards
3-inch M62 APC	98	90
3-inch T4 HVAP	157	135
17-pdr. APCBC	132	128
17-pdr. sabot	208	192
90mm M82 APC	129	122
90mm T30E16 HVAP	221	199

LEFT The driver in the M10 sat in the left front of the hull with the instrument panel to his left within the hull sponson. At the left of this picture can be seen the ends of the fiberboard packing tubes which contain the 3-inch gun ammunition. (US Army)

Design of the new 90mm turret began at Chevrolet but was shifted to Ford when it was determined that it would be built on the M10A1 chassis. Two soft steel prototypes of the T71 90mm GMC were ordered, and the first delivered in September 1943. An attempt by Ordnance to rush the design into production was rebuffed in September 1943 when it got mixed up in the controversy over 90mm gun tanks. Gen. Barnes from Ordnance continued to press the issue, and finally won AGF approval in October 1943. The T71 was seen as valuable in attacking fixed fortifications, and as a back-up in the event of German armor improvements. In October 1943, the AGF recommended that the T71 be manufactured to equip ten battalions and that M10 production be terminated since so many units were being converted to towed M5 3-inch guns. The Tank Destroyer Board continued to resist the T71 program and did not consider it suitable for use.

The trials proceeded quickly though several changes were recommended. The pilot had the turret anti-aircraft machine gun in a ring mount on the left side of the turret, much like the M18 tank destroyer. In January 1944, Ordnance recommended that this revert back to a simple pintle mount. The Armored Board recommended that the gun be fitted with a muzzle brake and employ long primer ammunition due to serious obscuration and flash problems from the existing gun. The Tank Destroyer Board conclusion that the M10A1 was automotively superior to the M10, combined with the availability of a significant reserve of M10A1 tank destroyers in storage in the United States after the departure of the tank destroyer battalions to Europe, led to the selection of the M10A1 chassis for future conversion. The original plan was to build 300 T71s, so the final batch of 300 M10A1 tank destroyers were completed without turrets in January 1944, specifically for this assignment. The AGF increased the requirement to 500 to provide an adequate reserve of vehicles, so the plan was amended to include conversion of surplus M10A1s.

Conversion of the 300 turretless M10A1 into the T71 configuration began at Grand Blanc in April 1944 when the first 25 were finished, and the final batch were finished in July 1944. The T71 was standardized on June 1 1944 as the 90mm Gun Motor Carriage M36. On May 15 1944, the requirement was increased to 600, and after the tank fighting in Normandy exposed the shortcomings of the M10, the total was increased to 1,400 on July 29 1944. The large increase caused some difficulties as only 913 M10A1 tank destroyers could be rounded up from training units and depots of the 1,413 that had been completed. As a result, it was decided to round out the production by mounting the remaining 187 turrets on M4A3 medium tank chassis. This version was later designated as the M36B1 and they were completed at Grand Blanc in October–December 1944.

A shortage of M10A1 chassis led the army to complete the production contract with M4A3 tank hulls since these were automotively identical to the M10A1. This version was designated the M36B1 and only 187 were converted from October to December 1944. The "x" shaped device over the turret is designed to support a canvas weather cover and was normally stowed on the forward turret roof. (US Army)

As Fisher's Grand Blanc facility was overwhelmed with work, the conversion program was spread out among other firms. Massey Harris was the first to be assigned a reconditioning and conversion (R&C) contract for 500 M36, and they were delivered between June 1944 and December 1944. American Locomotive converted 413 M10A1 tank destroyers into M36 tank destroyers between October and December 1944. The Army revised down the 1,400 vehicle objective for 1944 to 1,342. The 1945 program was originally set at a further 350 conversions, and gradually increased so that the grand total was finally set at 1,926. A final batch was converted by the Montreal Locomotive Works starting in May 1945, totaling 200 vehicles. In all these cases, the turrets were provided by Fisher. As a result, by the end of 1945, some 1,413 M36 90mm GMC were converted.

When the supply of M10A1 tank destroyers ran out, in January 1945 the Army decided to convert surplus M10s. This conversion was essentially the same as basic M36 except for the engine, and 672 M10s were reconditioned and converted into M36B2 tank destroyers at American Locomotive and 52 at Montreal Locomotive in 1945.

ABOVE **This view of the rear interior of the turret shows the ready racks for six rounds of 3-inch ammunition, in this case, all high explosive rounds. The rack to the left contains magazines for the vehicle's .45 cal. Thompson submachine gun which is stowed in the canvas bag under the rack. This is an early production vehicle, evident from the grouser stowage on the rear plate. (US Army)**

M36 AND M10C 17-PDR CONVERSIONS

	M36	M36B1	M36B2	M10C 17-pdr.
Apr 44	25			
May 44	100			98
Jun 44	120			81
Jul 44	155			69
Aug 44	100			70
Sep 44				112
Oct 44	75	50		126
Nov 44	290	93		152
Dec 44	348	44		82
Jan 45				86
Feb 45				95
Mar 45				30
Apr 45				16
May 45	10		50	
Post-war	190		674	
Total	**1,413**	**187**	**724**	**1,017**

LEFT **This view of the right side of the M10 turret shows the gun breech in the lower left, the indirect-fire artillery panoramic sight above it, and the two folding seats for the commander and assistant loader. The majority of the ammunition was stowed in black fiberboard shipping tubes in racks in the vehicle sponson, and can be seen here under the turret ring. (US Army)**

A variety of improvements were introduced on the M36 during conversion. The decision to begin fitting a heavy muzzle brake on the gun necessitated the design of a better equilibrator, a more powerful elevating mechanism and an improved travel lock. These features were fitted to all vehicles after the first 600 starting in early November 1944. Troops in the field had applied make-shift armored covers over the open roof of the M10 and M36, and a standardized roof armor kit was developed starting on August 15 1944 and was applied to late production vehicles. The M36 also underwent some of the other improvements more broadly applied to other M4 tank derivatives such as the spaced suspension of the M4E9 which permitted the use of extended end-connectors on both sides of the track. This gave the M36 better traction in mud and snow, and a portion of the M36 and M36B2 conversions undertaken in 1945 had these features incorporated during the conversion process.

COMBAT IN FRANCE

At the time of the Normandy landings in June 1944, there were 30 tank destroyer battalions in theater of which eleven were the new towed type and the rest were M10 or M18 self-propelled battalions. In May 1944, Army Ground Forces asked the headquarters of the European Theater of Operations US Army (ETOUSA) if they wanted any of the new M36 tank destroyers, and they were told that there was no need as the M10 was believed to be entirely adequate.

The original plan was to deploy the towed battalions on a scale of one per infantry division, and to retain the self-propelled battalions in corps and army reserve in keeping with tank destroyer doctrine. M10 tank destroyer battalions were committed to the fighting in France beginning on D-Day with several units landing in the later waves. There was very little tank fighting in the American sector, and the first tank knocked out by an M10 occurred only on June 23 when a PzKpfw III was hit by an M10 from B Co., 899th TD Battalion. In spite of the relative lack of armor encounters, the infantry commanders began requesting that more of the M10 battalions be attached to their divisions in place of the towed battalions. The towed 3-inch gun immediately proved to be a liability since it could not be used to provide direct fire support in the dense hedgerow country typical of the Normandy area, the armor on the gun was too thin to offer protection when the gun was deployed in forward positions, and once emplaced, the gun was very hard to move in normal battlefield conditions. In contrast, the M10 proved to be an extremely useful fire support weapon.

Although tank destroyer doctrine called for the concentration of the M10s in reserve groups, this policy was completely ignored in the European Theater of Operations (ETO) after June 1944 as being hopelessly unrealistic. German armor seldom attacked in massed quantities in the American sector of Normandy. After the first few weeks of fighting, the practice became to deploy one tank destroyer battalion with each infantry division to provide fire support. The infantry divisions were already allotted a tank bat-

As was the case with M10 units, M36 units also began to add partial or full roof armor to their vehicles, like this early production M36 of the 628th Tank Destroyer Battalion in Rheydt, Germany, on March 1 1945, during Operation Grenade. (US Army)

Although initially rejected by the Tank Destroyer Command before D-Day, the M36 was rushed into service in the fall of 1944 when it became evident that the M10 could not handle the German Panther tank in a frontal engagement. This is from the first batch of 40 vehicles which arrived in France in September to train tank destroyer crews. The M36s were converted from reconditioned M10A1 hulls, and this particular example is based on an M10A1 hull manufactured in the late summer of 1943 by which time the bosses for appliqué armor on the hull side had been deleted. (US Army)

talion, but it was soon found that a single battalion did not provide enough armored support for a division. The tank destroyer battalion augmented the tank battalion, and when not used in the direct fire role, also augmented the divisional field artillery by providing an additional source of indirect fire support. In practice, the divisions often split up the tank destroyer battalion, committing a company of M10 tank destroyers with each rifle regiment. While the M10's 3-inch gun proved more than adequate in this role, the M10 was not well configured for the close-support role. In particular, its open roof left it vulnerable to sniper fire at longer ranges, and vulnerable to grenades and other fire at close ranges. In addition, its armor was thinner than that of the M4 medium tank, and so it was more vulnerable to German anti-tank weapons. The lack of a power traverse for the turret was a significant drawback in tank fighting, as it took nearly eighty seconds to traverse the turret 180 degrees. Regardless of these shortcomings, the M10 proved to be a very valuable and versatile vehicle when skillfully employed. A report by the commanding officer of the 5th Tank Destroyer Group in Normandy is illustrative of their successful role in the fighting:

"What is not in the field manuals on tank destroyer use is the effective support which they render to a fighting infantry at the time of actual combat. An infantryman has his fortitude well tested and the mere presence of self-propelled tank destroyers in his immediate vicinity give a tremendous shot of courage to the committed infantryman. For example, at Chambois (during the closing of the Falaise Gap in August 1944), an infantry battalion moved towards the town with utter fearlessness to enemy artillery, mortar, and small arms fire when accompanied by some M10s. However, the M10s were delayed in crossing a stream for about thirty-five minutes. During this time, the infantry battalion continued to their objective which dominated a roadway leading to Chambois. They fought infantry, they bazooka-ed some armored vehicles including three tanks on the road, but on realizing that the M10s weren't firing, they started a retirement. Leading the parade to the rear was a short lad known as 'Shorty'. Shorty in the lead was the first man to see a platoon of M10s who had finally gotten across the stream. Shorty took a good look at the M10s, turned around, and shouted to the other men, 'Hell boys, what are we retiring for, here comes the TDs!' The entire company in mass immediately reversed their direction and returned to their excellent positions, and to say they fought for the next few hours with unusual bravery is stating it mildly. The point I am trying to make is that the appearance and the knowledge that self-propelled tank-destroyers were at hand was a major reason that the infantry attained success and victory. Often many men die or suffer to retain or exploit IF the inspiration furnished by the presence of self-propelled tank destroyers is known. The towed guns can be just as brave and thoroughly trained, but they never give much 'oomph' to the fighting doughboy when the chips are really down."

The tank destroyer saw their heaviest commitment in the European Theater of Operations (ETO) following D-Day. These are a column of late production M10s with the duck-bill counterweights from Co. A, 684th Tank Destroyer Battalion, supporting First US Army operations in the outskirts of Aachen on October 14 1944, the first German city captured by Allied forces. Aachen was the first German city entered by Allied forces, and the fighting there was particularly intense. These vehicles have sand-bags on the glacis plate, an attempt to provide added protection against German panzerfaust anti-tank rockets. (US Army)

Encounters with the German Panther tank in June and early July proved disheartening. The 3-inch gun could not penetrate the glacis plate of the Panther, and the gun mantlet could only be penetrated at ranges of 200 yards or less. The glacis plate on the Panther was so steeply sloped that it had an effective armor thickness against front attack of 185mm of steel armor even though it was only 85mm thick. This created an urgent demand for a better anti-tank weapon on the tank destroyers. The heaviest tank fighting began on July 10 1944, when Panzer Lehr Division staged a counterattack near Isigny, attempting to drive a wedge through the American sector. It was the first large-scale encounter with the new Panther tank. By coincidence, the narrow road net used by the Panzer Lehr Division's Panther tank regiment near Le Desert ran through the sector covered by the 899th Tank Destroyer Battalion. As a result, there were a series of intense, close-range battles between the M10s and Panthers over a two-day period. Although the M10 had a great deal of difficulty penetrating the thick Panther frontal armor, it was far more vulnerable on its flanks, and could be defeated by the 3-inch gun at most combat ranges. In spite of the shortcomings of the 3-inch gun, the 899th Tank Destroyer Battalion was credited 12 Panthers, 1 PzKpfw IV and 1 StuG III, and played a central role in blunting the German attack. The tank destroyers took advantage of the hedgerow terrain, and much of the tank fighting took place at point blank ranges of under two hundred meters. The poor performance of the 3-inch gun against the Panther came as a shock to the tank destroyer crews, and a major controversy erupted over the lack of preparation for dealing with the new threat. As a test, a captured Panther tank was subjected to fire from a variety of US and British guns which only reinforced these conclusions.

The inadequate anti-tank capabilities of the M10 revealed by the Normandy tank fighting led to considerable pressure to field the new M36 tank destroyer with the 90mm gun as soon as possible, and on July 6 1944 ETOUSA cabled back to the United States asking that all M10 battalions be converted to M36 as soon as possible. Resistance to the M36 both from the tank destroyer battalions in Europe and the Tank Destroyer Board in the United States evaporated. By September 1944, after the experience of the summer fighting, the US 12th Army Group requested that of the 52 tank destroyer battalions committed to the

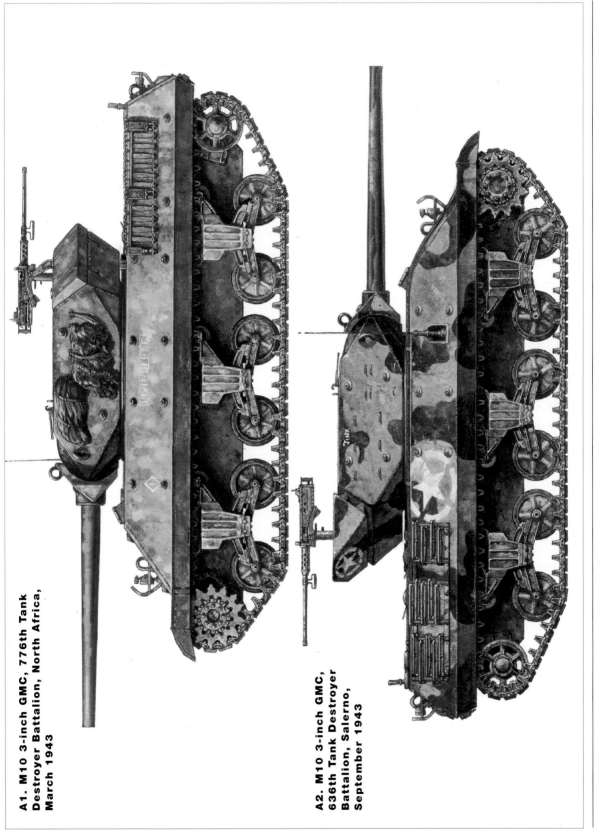

A1. M10 3-inch GMC, 776th Tank Destroyer Battalion, North Africa, March 1943

A2. M10 3-inch GMC, 636th Tank Destroyer Battalion, Salerno, September 1943

A

B

M10C 17-pdr. SPM, Canadian 4th Anti-Tank
Regiment, Eelde, Netherlands, May 1945

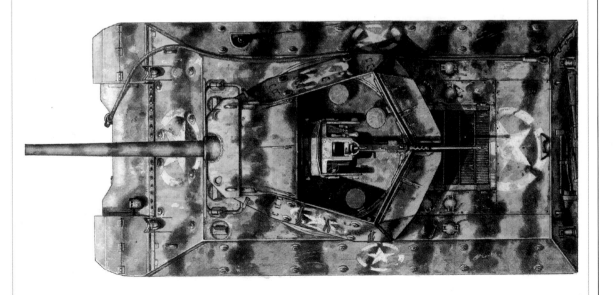

D. M10, US TANK DESTROYER BATTALION, 1944

KEY

1. Transmission cover
2. Tow cable
3. Turret traverse wheel
4. Lifting hook
5. Co-driver's periscope
6. Co-driver's hatch
7. Turret external stowage tie-downs
8. Gun mantlet
9. 3-inch gun barrel
10. Turret weather cover folding braces
11. Gun elevating wheel
12. Gun safety brace
13. Grenade stowage box
14. Indirect fire panoramic sight
15. 3-inch gun breech
16. M2 HB .50 cal. heavy machine gun
17. Rear weather cover folding brace
18. Turret counterweight
19. Gun travel brace
20. Engine access grill
21. Engine fuel covers
22. Appliqué armor attachment bolts
23. Rear lights
24. Crew folding seat
25. Idler wheel
26. Track grouser stowage
27. Suspension bogie
28. Turret ammunition ready rack
29. Track end connector
30. Hull sponson ammunition stowage
31. Turret floor stowage cover
32. Electrical conduit to turret
33. Crew folding seat
34. Forward hull floor stowage
35. Driver's seat
36. Transmission
37. Vehicle siren
38. Front headlight
39. Drive sprocket
40. T51 rubber block track

SPECIFICATION

Crew: 5 (commander, gunner, loader, driver, co-driver)

Combat weight: 32.6 tons

Power-to-weight ratio: 12.6 hp/T

Overall length: 22.3 ft.

Width: 10 ft.

Height: 9.5 ft.

Engine: Two General Motors 6046 12 cylinder, 2 cycle diesel with 850 cubic inch displacement; 410hp

Transmission: Syncromesh transmission with 5 forward, one reverse gear

Fuel capacity: 165 gallons

Max. speed (road): 30mph

Max. speed (cross-country): 20mph

Max. range: 200 miles

Fuel consumption: 1.2 miles per gallon

Ground clearance: 17 inches

Armament: 3-inch gun M7 in Mount M5; .50 cal. M2 HB machine gun

Main gun ammunition: 54 rounds 3-inch; 1,000 rounds .50 cal.

M62 APC projectile: muzzle velocity 2,600 ft/sec; penetration of 93mm at 500 yards at 30 degrees

M93 HVAP projectile: muzzle velocity 3,400 ft/sec; penetration of 157mm at 500 yards at 30 degrees

Max. effective range: 16,100 yards

Gun depression/elevation: -10 to + 30 degrees

Armor: 57mm gun mantlet; 25mm turret sides; 38mm upper hull front; 50mm lower hull front; 19mm upper hull side; 25mm lower hull side

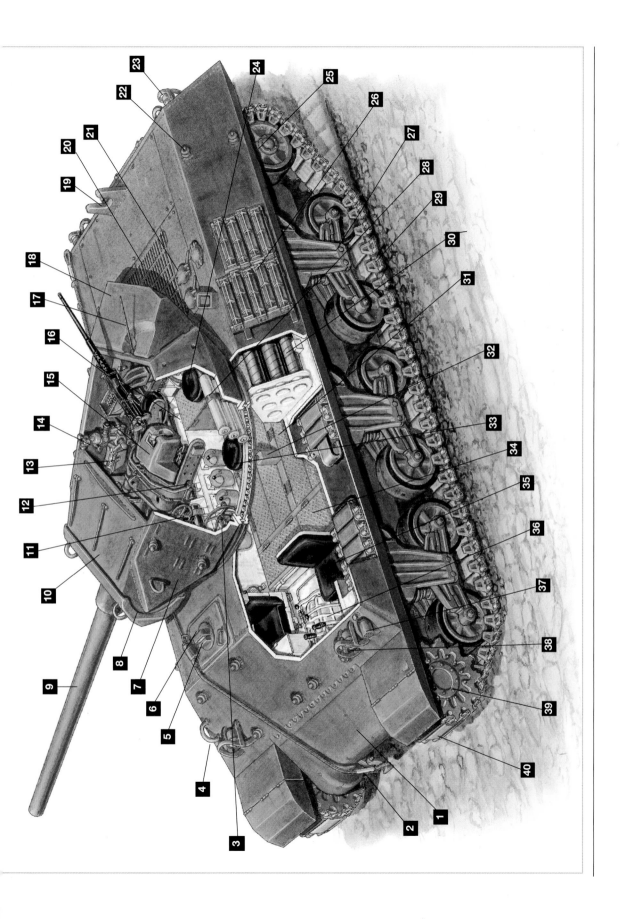

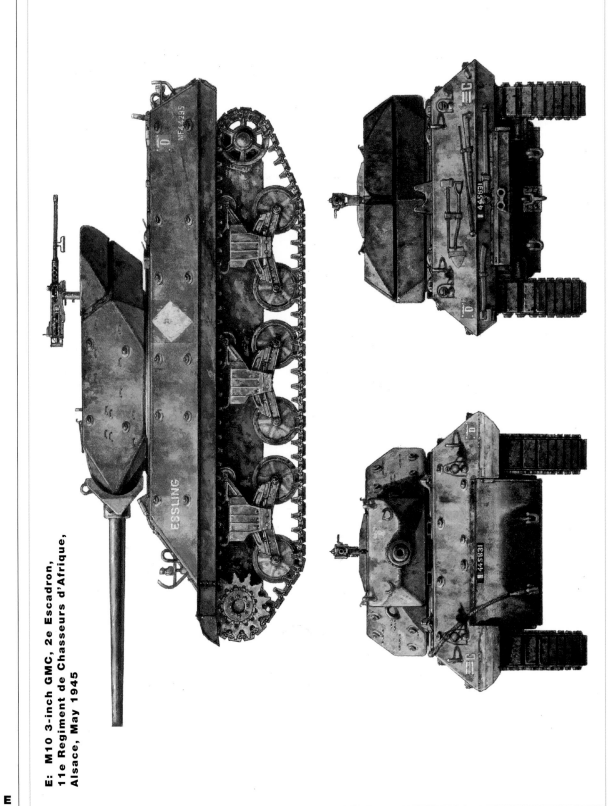

**E: M10 3-inch GMC, 2e Escadron,
11e Regiment de Chasseurs d'Afrique,
Alsace, May 1945**

E

F1: M36 90mm GMC, Regiment Blinde Colonial d'Extreme Orient, Tonkin, Indochina, 1953

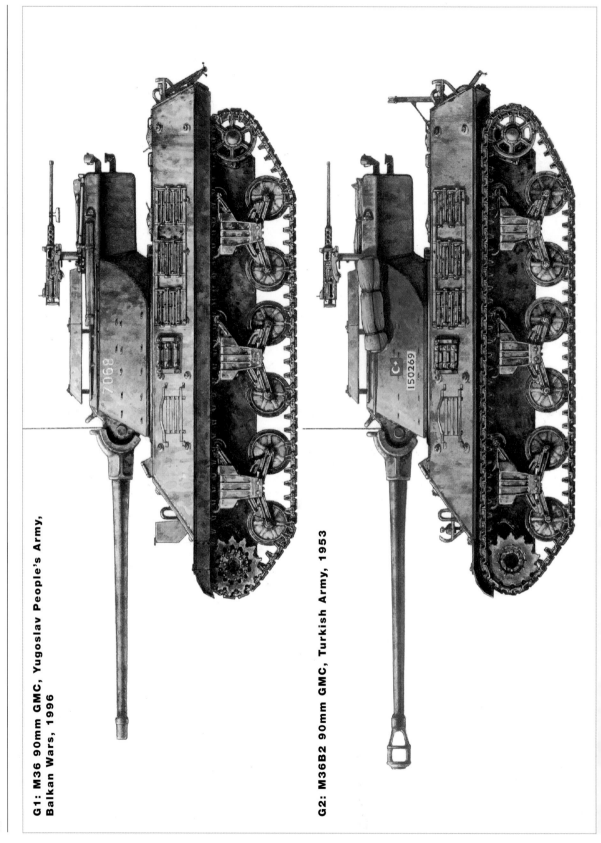

G

G1: M36 90mm GMC, Yugoslav People's Army, Balkan Wars, 1996

G2: M36B2 90mm GMC, Turkish Army, 1953

theater, 20 be converted to M36, 20 retain the M10 or M18 and the remaining 12 remain as towed battalions, but completely reequipped with the new T5E1 90mm anti-tank gun. In practice, the changes were not so well organized.

The first forty M36 tank destroyers arrived in France in the first week of September 1944 and were issued to the First US Army. After preparation and crew training, they first went into action in October 1944 during the fighting along the German border. Due to the small numbers originally available, it was not possible to equip entire battalions with the M36. As a result, the initial practice was to issue it to existing M10 battalions, usually on a scale of one company at a time. As more became available, entire battalions were reequipped.

The general conclusion was that the M36 was a definite improvement over the M10 when dealing with the Panther tank, though it was not the complete solution. The existing 90mm ammunition would not reliably penetrate the Panther glacis plate at ranges over 500 yards. Crews found that it was better to target the turret, which was more vulnerable. In some circumstances, it was found that several 90mm rounds fired in rapid succession at the glacis would penetrate, presumably due to the collapse of the armor when partial penetrations were hit again by another round. The Panther was far more vulnerable when hit from the side. In an engagement with a Panther at 1500 yards by an M36 of the 776th TD Battalion north of Shalback, "Two hits were scored on the tank: one in the track by AP which blew the track off, and the other round of AP in the turret which blew a hole about 6 inches in diameter and made cracks in the entire right side of the turret. The seams on the back deck were also ripped. The round went into the turret, blew the breech block off, then blew off about half the turret top." New ammunition, better able to make frontal penetrations, was in demand by the crews.

As the tank destroyer battalions gained more experience with their M10 and M36 vehicles, they began to modify them to overcome deficiencies. As in the case of US Army tank units, some tank destroyer battalions began to add sand-bags to the hull front to provide a measure of added protection against German anti-tank rockets like the panzerfaust that were encountered frequently when supporting infantry. One of the most glaring deficiencies in the M10 and M36 was the lack of a co-axial or hull machine gun to engage German infantry. The

Although the M10 hull was fitted with bosses for attaching appliqué armor, no armor kits were ever designed or manufactured. Some units added their own improvised appliqué armor, like this intermediate production M10 of the 899th Tank Destroyer Battalion having a road-wheel replaced during a lull in the fighting in Weiler, Germany, on November 27 1944. (US Army)

location of the .50 cal. anti-aircraft machine gun at the rear of the turret was nearly useless. Some units began to remount this weapon on the front left corner of the turret to permit its use against infantry. Many units found the open roof of the M10 and M36 to be a mixed blessing. On the one hand, it provided good visibility when looking for targets, and it offered an easy means of escape if the vehicle was hit and burning. On the other hand, it made the crew

The first M36 tank destroyers retained the simple stirrup gun rest on the rear hull roof. This was eventually replaced with a folding travel lock as seen on this vehicle from a tank destroyer battalion in Patton's Third Army operating in Luxembourg in the final phase of the Battle of the Bulge on January 3 1945. It is receiving a hasty camouflage of whitewash to better adapt it to winter conditions. (US Army)

more vulnerable to sniper fire and artillery air bursts. Some tank destroyer units in Italy began to experiment with armored covers in the summer of 1944, and the idea also caught on in France. In September 1944, the 813th Tank Destroyer Battalion had its maintenance personnel attach improvised ⁵/₈ inch steel folding covers over the turret roof of about half of its M10 tank destroyers to provide a measure of protection. This led to a parallel program in the United States, with Ordnance authorizing the start of a program to develop an overhead cover for the M10 on September 13 1944. In November 1944, the commander of the 5th Tank Destroyer Group responsible for the battalions in the Seventh US Army in Alsace queried all his battalions on the matter but found that with the exception of the 813th TD Battalion, none of the other battalions thought the added armor was worth the trouble. This attitude would soon change.

The M10 and M36 battalions had the same mobility problems as the M4 medium tank battalions due to the unusually wet autumn and the resulting mud. As in the case of the tanks, extended end connectors, popularly called duck-bills, were added to the tracks. This caused more problems on the tank destroyers due to the tendency of the duck-bills to catch on the hull underhang. In some units, the underhang was completely cut off when the duck-bill were attached, but other battalions found that by trimming the area above the rear idler and removing the front fenders, the rest of the armor could be left in place.

One of the most important improvements in M10 performance was the gradual supply of a new type of ammunition. The T4 high velocity armor piercing (HVAP) 3-inch projectile used a tungsten carbide core, and had markedly superior anti-armor performance to the more conventional M62 AP ammunition. It was able to penetrate the Panther's mantlet at 1,000 yards compared to only about 200 yards for the older M62 projectile. The first 2,000 rounds of T4 ammunition for the 3-inch and 76mm guns were air delivered in August 1944, but in fact did not become widely available until November 1944. Initial field trials of the ammunition found that its penetration performance was inferior to the British 17-pdr. gun but that it was more accurate. In September 1944,

The self-propelled tank destroyer battalions proved so superior to the towed battalions during the fighting in the Ardennes in December 1944–January 1945, that the towed battalions were hastily reequipped in the ensuing months. This M10 belonged to the highest scoring unit, the 773rd Tank destroyer Battalion, which was credited with 103 German tanks and assault guns through the Battle of the Bulge, and 132 by March 1945. This particular M10, commanded by Sgt. Jacob Kretchik, was credited with five German tanks during the Ardennes fighting. (US Army)

BELOW The 813th Tank Destroyer Battalion pioneered the development of overhead roof armor to protect the turret crew from snipers. Two types were developed, including this partial roof that covered only the forward section of the turret and was more common on M10s with the intermediate turret with wedge counterweights. This M10 was seen in Soultz, France, on January 14 1945, following the repulse of the German Operation Nordwind offensive in Alsace. (US Army)

ETOUSA headquarters cabled back to the United States that they needed 43,000 rounds evenly split between 3-inch and 76mm guns, by January 1945, and 10,000 rounds monthly after that. However, tungsten was in such short supply that through early March 1945, only about 18,000 rounds arrived in Europe, including about 10,500 rounds for the M10 tank destroyers.

The scale of tank fighting tapered off dramatically after September 1944 due to the heavy German losses in Normandy and Lorraine. As a result, there was less pressure to accelerate the fielding of the M36. By the time of the Battle of the Bulge in December 1944, the M36 was still substantially outnumbered by the M10 tank destroyer. By January 1945, there were six M36 battalions in service, five with the 12th US Army Group, and one with the 6th US Army Group. The Battle of the Bulge saw a renewed commitment of German tank strength in the West, not only increased numbers of Panthers, but heavy tanks such as the King Tiger. The inadequate performance of the 3-inch gun on the M10 and a shortage of HVAP ammunition led to renewed pressure to accelerate replacement with the M36. In addition, the towed anti-tank guns once again proved to be far inferior to the self-propelled battalions. As a result, the Army decided to completely replace all towed battalions. The pattern was often to replace M10s with M36s in the existing self-propelled battalions, and then convert the towed battalions with the redundant M10s. The Ardennes fighting and the related fighting in Alsace also changed attitudes about other issues. For example, the battalions of the 5th Tank Destroyer Group which had previously been so skeptical of armored roof covers, completely changed their attitude and a program began to provide covers for all vehicles. There was also added pressure to field more HVAP ammunition

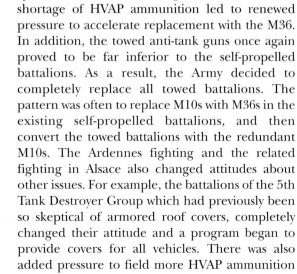

for the 3-inch and 90mm guns. The new T30E16 90mm HVAP ammunition for the M36 gun finally gave the tank destroyers the ability to penetrate the glacis plate at a range of about 450 yards and started to become available in January 1945.

Although the number of encounters with German panzers trailed off dramatically after the Ardennes fighting due to the heavy German losses, an increasing number of heavily armored German vehicles were encountered. The heaviest of all was the Jagdtiger, the largest and most powerful armored vehicle of World War II, armed with a 128mm gun. The sch. Pz.Jg. Abt. 653 was the first unit equipped with this monster, and it was deployed at the end of December 1944 to support the 17.SS Pz. Gren. Div. during Operation Nordwind in the Alsace region. On 5 January 1945, a few Jagdtigers, accompanied by a captured M4 medium tank, supported the panzergrenadiers during an attack near Rimling. The armored elements of the German battle group occupied hull-down positions outside the town but did not notice when an M36 from the 776th Tank Destroyer Battalion carefully moved into a flanking position. At a range of 900 yards, the M36 put a single armor-piercing round into the side of Jagdtiger number 134, causing an internal ammunition fire which destroyed the vehicle in a catastrophic explosion, blowing off the superstructure sides. The M36 then engaged the captured M4 medium tank being used by the Germans, and put it out

The other type of armored roof developed by the 813th Tank Destroyer Battalion extended all the way to the rear, and had folding panels in the center. This pattern was more common on late production turrets with the enlarged rear and duck-bill counterweights. (US Army)

US ARMY M10 AND M36 STRENGTH AND LOSSES IN THE ETO 1944-45*

	M10 Strength	M36 Strength	M10 Losses	M36 Losses
June 1944	691	-	1	-
July 1944	743	-	17	-
August 1944	758	-	28	-
September 1944	763	-	40	-
October 1944	486	170	71	2
November 1944	573	183	45	5
December 1944	790	236	62	21
January 1945	760	365	69	26
February 1945	686	826	106	18
March 1945	684	884	27	21
April 1945	427	1,054	37	34
May 1945	427	1,029	37	25

*Data as of the 20th of each month

of action. The M36 then began engaging the panzergrenadiers with high explosive fire. The battle-group withdrew, thinking that the Jagdtiger had been destroyed by an unseen bazooka crew. The Jagdtiger was plagued by mechanical unreliability, and it was seldom encountered in combat again.

US ARMY TANK BATTALIONS IN THE ETO APRIL 15 1945

1st Army		3rd Army		9th Army	
Battalion	Type	Battalion	Type	Battalion	Type
612	M18	602	M18	605	M5
629	M36	603	M18	628	M36
630	M36	607	M36	638	M18
634	M10	609	M18	643	M18
644	M10	610	M36	654	M36
656	M36	631	M5	702	M36
661	M18	635	M5	771	M36
692	M36	691	M36	772	M36
703	M36	704	M18	801	M18
814	M36	705	M18	802	M36
817	M18	773	M10	807	M18
820	M18	803	M36	809	M18
893	M10	811	M18	813	M36
899	M36	818	M36	821	M10
		808	M36	823	M10

12th Army Group		Reserve 15th Army	
825	M5	774	M36

TANK DESTROYERS IN THE PACIFIC

The tank destroyers were not well suited to the type of fighting encountered in the Pacific, but seven battalions saw service there on a limited scale, all but one equipped with the M10. The M10 was first used in combat in the Pacific on Kwajelin in support of the 7th Division, but as substitute equipment in a tank battalion. The first combat use of tank destroyer battalions in the Pacific was in the Palaus Islands in June 1944 with M10s of the 819th Tank Destroyer Battalion. The most extensive use of tank destroyers took place in the Philippines campaign with three tank destroyer battalions taking part in the fighting on Luzon (632nd, 637th, 640th) and later on Leyte (632nd Tank Destroyer Battalion). Due to the small numbers of Japanese tanks, M10 tank destroyers were used almost exclusively for direct fire support of infantry. In general, the tank destroyers were not well received in the Pacific, as their open tops exposed them to the ferocious Japanese close-in anti-armor tactics.

THE M10 IN BRITISH SERVICE

As in the case of so many American armored vehicles, Britain became the most important Lend Lease recipient of the M10 GMC. The first thousand were ordered in 1943. A total of 1,128 vehicles were delivered in 1944, and a further 520 in 1945, for a grand total of 1,648, though some sources indicate the total was 1,654. The M10 in British service was called the 3" SPM (self-propelled mount) M10 Mk I

with the heavy wedge counterweight and 3" SPM M10 Mk II with the duck-bill counterweight.

Britain had been working on a new 17-pdr. anti-tank gun to deal with the threat of new German tanks, and so not surprisingly there was some immediate interest in mounting it in the M10 in lieu of the 3-inch anti-tank gun. As mentioned earlier, the M10 gun mount had been designed from the outset to permit an easy substitution of other guns including the 17-pdr. and the US 105mm howitzer. As a result, the British conversions were not difficult. Indeed, much of the work was connected with secondary issues including ammunition stowage, and British pattern radios and stowage. Most of the conversions were undertaken on the later M10 with duck-bill counterweights due to the better balance of the turret. The conversions began in the spring of 1944 at the Royal Ordnance Factory in Leeds, and the first 98 were converted in May 1944. From May 1944 to April 1945, 1,017 M10s were converted, though there is some evidence that additional vehicles were converted in tank troop workshops. They were variously designated as M10C or M10 17-pdr.

There has been a long-standing controversy over why the US Army didn't adopt the 17-pdr. gun for both its M4 tanks and M10 tank destroyers as it had done earlier in the war with the 6-pdr. While it has often been charged that the reason was the "not-invented-here" syndrome, the principal reason was that until June 1944, the US Army mistakenly believed that its existing anti-tank guns were adequate to deal with the German tank threat. The British Army had experienced the continual escalation of armor thickness and gun power since 1940, and wisely moved to the more powerful 17-pdr. gun in 1944 even without a specific appreciation of the problems that the

An M36 of the 703rd Tank Destroyer Battalion moves past a German PzKpfw IV knocked out in the Ardennes fighting near Langlir, Belgium. This vehicle is fitted with the improved M3 90mm gun which was threaded for a muzzle brake and fitted with a thread protector. It was planned to retrofit vehicles with muzzle brakes, but few arrived before the war ended. This vehicle also has one of the standard field expedients for M36 tank destroyers, a .50 cal. machine gun repositioned on a pintle mount on the left front corner of the turret. (US Army)

Panther tank would present. Most of the institutions of the US Army lacked the experience to appreciate the dynamics of tank armor and tank gun development, and were reluctant to introduce yet another gun and its associated family of ammunition into the already strained logistical network. By the fall of 1944, the US Army already had six types of anti-tank gun ammunition in service (37mm, 57mm, 75mm, 76mm, 3-inch, 90mm). By the time that the problems with the 3-inch gun became apparent in the summer of 1944, the 90mm gun and HVAP ammunition were ready even though their deployment had been delayed by US Army indifference.

In general, the M10 and M10C were issued to Royal Artillery anti-tank regiments in the armoured divisions, or independent regiments attached at corps level. Regiments with infantry divisions tended to use the 17-pdr. Archer on the Valentine chassis, though there were exceptions. The usual regimental organization was four batteries consisting of a battery of M10 3-inch, a battery with M10 17-pdr. and two towed anti-tank gun batteries. The towed batteries in Italy still had the 6-pdr. gun in 1944, but the towed batteries in Normandy had been reequipped with the 17-pdr. Both self-propelled and towed batteries had twelve guns each. Besides service in British units, the M10 was also provided to armies supplied through British channels including the Canadian, Polish, New Zealand, and South African forces.

The M10s were first committed to combat in Italy and were in action by the spring of 1944. As the Italian theater was not given priority, the first M10Cs were not delivered until August 1944, and by mid-September, there were only 30 in service. By November, this total had risen to 152 17-pdr. M10s. A total of nine anti-tank regiments of the Eighth Army and Commonwealth units of the Fifth Army employed the M10 and M10C during the Italian campaign. This included four British regiments, two Polish regiments, and single Canadian, South African, and New Zealand regiments.

Both the M10 and M10C were deployed immediately during the Normandy campaign, and at least seven regiments were in action with the 21st Army Group by July 1944, and fifteen by 1945. The 17-pdr. was the most effective Allied anti-tank weapon of the Normandy campaign, and the only one able to effectively deal with the Panther tank. The 17-pdr. when firing the basic armor-piercing APCBC ammunition could not reliably penetrate the Panther glacis plate, but it could penetrate the gun mantlet at 1,250 yards compared to about 200 yards for the 3-inch gun on the unmodified M10. In the late summer, an improved discarding sabot ammunition began to arrive which further boosted 17-pdr. performance.

However, this sabot ammunition proved to have erratic accuracy, and during a series of field trials in France in August 1944, only about three out of five rounds hit the target compared to all rounds of the normal armor-piercing ammunition. This problem was due in part to manufacturing problems with the propellant, and was gradually improved in 1944–45. Curiously enough, it was an M10-C 17-pdr. SPM of the 75th Anti-Tank Regiment that was the first British armored vehicle to fire into Germany during 11th Armoured Division operations near the frontier in October 1944.

By the spring of 1945, there were about 420 M10Cs with the 21st Army Group of which nearly 300 were in unit service. Of these, about 120 were with five Canadian regiments, 24 with a single Polish regiment, and the remainder with nine British regiments.

OTHER LEND-LEASE USE

The second largest operator of the M10 other than British and Commonwealth units was the Free French army which was actually the first to receive the type in 1943. In total, some 155 M10s were delivered to French units through Lend-Lease channels though about a hundred additional M10 tank destroyers were transferred from US Army stocks to the French First Army during the war when it was part of the Sixth US Army Group.

In contrast to the US tank destroyer battalions, the initial French regiments had five M10s in each platoon instead of four, so that regimental strength was 45 instead of 36 M10s. The first four regiments were organized in the summer of 1943, the 7e, 8e, 9, and 11e Regiments des Chasseurs d'Afrique (RCA) in this heavy configuration, later called "type no. 1". It was subsequently decided to organize the remaining regiments along the lines of American tank destroyer battalions with 36 M10s each, called "type no. 2". Only two regiments, the 7e and 8e RCA in Italy, retained the heavy configuration. By January 1944, the plan had been increased to eight regiments, three attached to armored divisions and five organic to army corps. In fact, through 1944, only seven regiments were in service with the eighth not raised until 1945.

The first French M10 unit into action was the 7e RCA which was deployed near Mt. Molino in Italy in January 1944. Probably the best known of the French M10 units was also the most unusual, the Regiment Blinde des Fusiliers Marins (RBFM) which was organic to

The M10 also saw limited service in the Pacific theater. The crew of this late production M10 of the 632nd Tank Destroyer Battalion does maintenance of their vehicle at Ormoc bay on Leyte in the Philippines on December 16 1944. The remnants of a wading trunk can be seen on the rear which provided air supply to the vehicle engine when coming ashore from landing ships through deep water during the initial invasion. (US Army)

LeClerc's legendary 2nd Armored Division. Due to a shortage of army volunteers, the regiment was formed from French Navy sailors, who retained their distinctive caps. This unit was involved in the liberation of Paris where one of its M10s engaged in a duel with a Panther on the Place de la Concorde in the heart of the city. The regiment later distinguished itself in the fighting in Lorraine in September 1944, particularly the destruction of

The most effective version of the M10 was the British M10C 17-pdr. which had the 3-inch gun replaced by the 17-pdr. This M10C is seen in training with the Polish 1st Anti-Tank Regiment in the UK prior to deployment to Normandy with the Polish 1st Armoured Division. (Sikorski Institute)

Panzer Brigade 112 at Dompaire. This unit served initially with Patton's Third Army during the summer of 1944, but later was attached to the Seventh US Army during the fighting in Alsace. All the other regiments served with the First French Army, attached to the Sixth US Army Group in Alsace in the fall and autumn of 1944. Of the 227 M10s known to have served in the French regiments, at least 47 were lost in combat.

The Sixth US Army Group considered equipping some French regiments with the M36 in 1945, but this was rejected as all French tank destroyer battalions were self-propelled while several US battalions in this command were still towed and had yet to be converted.

The only other Lend-Lease recipient of the M10 during the war was the Soviet Union where some 52 M10s were shipped in 1943. These were used to form two self-propelled artillery regiments (SAP) in 1944. The 1239th SAP, with 10 M10s, was attached to the 16th Tank Corps, 2nd Tank Army during the summer campaigns in Byelorussia and Poland. It fought alongside the 1441st SAP, equipped with the SU-85, during fighting in central Poland in July–August 1944. The 1223rd SAP of the 29th Tank Corps, 5th Guards Tank Army took part in the summer 1944 campaigns in Byelorussia, the Baltic region, and East Prussia. By the end of the war, it had been reduced in strength to ten M10s.

POSTWAR USE

In the wake of the wartime controversy, the US Army disbanded the tank destroyer battalions, favoring the use of better armed tanks for the same mission. Most M10s were scrapped, although small numbers of M10s were exported to Italy and other allies, and the British M10C 17-pdr. vehicles were provided in small numbers to Denmark, the Netherlands, and Belgium. Britain also provided a small number of M10C 17-pdrs to Egypt, and they served in the 1948 and 1956 wars against Israel. Britain continued to use its M10C 17-pdr. tank destroyers until the mid-1950s as did France.

The M36 remained a viable tank killer well into the 1950s. During the Korean War crisis of 1950, a shortage developed of the M26 and M46 tanks. As a result, the M36 became one of the preferred armored vehicles for MAP (Military Assistance Program) transfers. South Korean tank battalions were provided with about 110 M36s and a small number of M10 tank destroyers during the war where they formed the seed of Korea's new armored force. Other NATO allies also received the M36 including France, Belgium, Italy, and Turkey until modern tanks such as the M47 became available. In November 1950, the French Army deployed the Regiment Blinde Colonial d'Extreme Orient (RBCEO) to Indochina with the M36B2 as there were fears that China might intervene with its IS-2 heavy tanks. Although intended to provide anti-tank defense, the absence of armored vehicles in Viet-minh hands meant that the RBCEO was used mainly to provide fire support for French Army units in the Tonkin region of northern Vietnam during the Indochina fighting.

Another recipient of the M36B2 was Pakistan which deployed them in armoured regiments due to shortages of the M47 and M48 tank. At least two regiments still had these in service during the 1965 war with India, the 11 Cavalry and the 13 Lancers. These regiments had two squadrons of Patton tanks each and a squadron with the M36B2. The other armoured regiments in the infantry divisions were also supposed to have M36B2s, but there were too few to fill out the order of battle.

One of the largest recipients of the M36 in the early 1950s was the Yugoslav People's Army which received the M36 and M36B1. These remained in service through the 1990s, though by this time many vehicles had become so worn-out that their engines were replaced with the V-55 diesel from the Soviet T-55 tank. They were used extensively by Serbian and Croatian units during the Balkans civil war.

The M10C 17-pdr. was one of the few Allied armored vehicles in Normandy able to cope with the German Panther tank, the other being the Sherman Firefly also equipped with the 17-pdr. anti-tank gun. This M10C served with the 91st Anti-Tank Regiment in Normandy, and having been raised from Scottish infantry units, carried Scottish names like this one, Glengarry II. (NARA)

The first Allied units to receive the M10 were Free French regiments raised by the French First Army in North Africa in 1943, with US assistance. These two M10s of the 7e Regiment des Chasseurs d'Afrique are seen on parade in Casablanca before deployment to Italy. (NARA)

BIBLIOGRAPHY

There is no published history of the M10 and M36, though there is coverage in many survey accounts of US tank destroyers and the Sherman tank. There are several very good accounts of the trials and tribulations of the Tank Destroyer force including Charles Baily's *Faint Praise: American Tanks and Tank Destroyers during World War II* (Archon, 1983); Christopher Gabel's *Seek, Strike and Destroy: US Army Tank Destroyer Doctrine in World War II* (US Army CGSC, 1985); and Lonnie Gill's *Tank Destroyer Forces-WWII* (Turner, 1992). This account was based primarily on original reports and unpublished Ordnance histories. These included Anne Jones' postwar history for the Ordnance Dept. *Record of Army Ordnance R&D: 3-Inch Gun Motor Carriages*; numerous reports of the Tank Destroyer Board; Tank-Automotive Center; Ordnance Dept.; Requirements Division, US Army Ground Forces; and various Army Service Forces reports. Sources on the service history of these vehicles were found in reports of the Observers Groups sent to the Mediterranean and European Theater of Operations, as well as postwar studies such as Lt.Col. Emory Dunham's *Tank Destroyer History* for the AGF Historical Section in 1946, and the 1945 General Board report *Study of Organization, Equipment, and Tactical Employment of Tank Destroyer Units* which led to the disbandment of the tank destroyer force. Other operational records that were consulted included those of the AFV&W Section of the 6th Army Group, and various headquarters records of ETOUSA and the US 12th Army Group. These records were found primarily at the US National Archives and Records Administration (NARA) in College Park, Maryland, and the US Army Military History Institute (MHI) at the US Army War College, Carlisle Barracks, Pennsylvania.

The M10 was used by more armies in the Italian theater than anywhere else. Canada employed them in Italy with the 4th Anti-Tank Regiment of the 5th Canadian Armoured Division, and a heavily camouflaged example is seen here during operations near Montevarchi in 1944. (NARA)

COLOR PLATE COMMENTARY

A1. M10 3-INCH GMC, 776TH TANK DESTROYER BATTALION, NORTH AFRICA, MARCH 1943

During the campaign in Tunisia, the normal US Army olive drab finish proved too dark for camouflage purposes in the local desert setting. So many armored vehicles had an improvised camouflage scheme applied using local mud daubed on using whatever means were available. The yellow star marking is partially obscured by the camouflage. This vehicle has a name, Invincible, crudely chalked on the hull side. Towards the front is a number "1" in a diamond, the significance of which is not clear as it is not a typical US Army style of tactical marking.

A2. M10 3-INCH GMC, 636TH TANK DESTROYER BATTALION, SALERNO, SEPTEMBER 1943

The first "ace" M10 tank destroyer was the vehicle commanded by Sgt. Edwin Yosts which knocked out five PzKpfw IV tanks, a half-track, and a German pillbox in a 25-minute battle in the Salerno bridgehead during a German counter-attack on September 14 1943. The M10 was nicknamed "Jinx" and the name can be seen in small letters near the top of the turret side. The camouflage finish is a very irregular pattern of black over the usual olive drab. The markings are the enlarged circle around the US star which had been prescribed starting with the Sicily campaign earlier in the year after North African experiences had found that the star alone could be mistaken for a German cross at long ranges.

B. M10C 17-PDR. SPM, CANADIAN 4TH ANTI-TANK REGIMENT, EELDE, NETHERLANDS, MAY 1945

Canadian vehicles, like most Commonwealth armour, tended to follow British markings practices. The M10, since it was considered an artillery vehicle, carries the British style of artillery unit insignia centrally on the bow and hull side which identifies it as the first vehicle of C Troop. On the bow is the

Another Commonwealth M10 operator in Italy was South Africa, and these belong to the 1/11th Anti-Tank Regiment of the 6th South African Armoured Division near Porretta on November 17 1944. The two vehicles in the foreground are late production examples without the appliqué armor bosses on the hull side. Britain also supplied Lend-Lease M10s to New Zealand and Polish units in Italy. (US Army)

arms of service insignia, a white 77 on a blue and red square, identifying the 4th Anti-Tank Regiment within the Canadian 5th Armoured Division. The divisional insignia, a yellow maple leaf on a maroon square, is on the opposite side. The vehicle name, Chippawa, is seen on the hull side and on the bow in white, along with the registration number in white. British and Canadian vehicles were finished either in the original olive drab, or its British equivalent, Shade No. 15 olive drab, which replaced Standard Camouflage Colour No. 2 khaki brown in 1944. This color was very similar to US olive drab, and was adopted to avoid the need to repaint US Lend-Lease vehicles.

C. M10 3-INCH GMC, 894TH TANK DESTROYER BATTALION, ANZIO, FEBRUARY 1944

The 894th Tank Destroyer Battalion painted its vehicles in a distinctive camouflage scheme of narrow bands of black sprayed over the normal olive drab finish. This scheme was locally called "tiger stripes", and was used on a number of the unit's vehicles. This vehicle is typical of M10s in the Italian theater where large numbers of national identity markings were common. This vehicle has stars in all standard locations.

D. M10, US TANK DESTROYER BATTALION, 1944

(see plate for full details)

ABOVE **Following the war, some M36 tank destroyers were upgraded with roof armor and the new M3A1 gun. With M26 and M46 tanks in short supply during the Korean War, these refurbished M36 tank destroyers were offered to US allies to give them the heavy firepower needed to deal with Soviet tanks. Several South Korean tank units were equipped with the M36 during the Korean War like the one seen here with the 53rd Tank Company in 1953. (US Army)**

BELOW **The final variant of the M36 series, the M36B2, was also supplied to several armies after World War II. This version was based on the M10 chassis, but the conversions took place in 1945 when several other upgrades had been developed including the so-called "E9" suspension which space the bogies out from the hull to permit the use of extended end-connectors on both sides of the track. These M36B2s belong to a Turkish Army unit on display in 1953. (US Army)**

ABOVE **The final production batches of the M36 starting in November 1944 were fitted with muzzle brakes like this vehicle seen at Aberdeen Proving Ground in December 1944. This vehicle was converted from a late production M10A1 chassis lacking the bosses for appliqué on the hull side. (US Army)**

BELOW **Since the M36 and M36B1 were automotively identical, they were often deployed in the same units. This M36 battalion is seen supporting 7th Army operations along the Maine River in Germany in April 1945. An M36B1 can be seen at the rear of the column while M36 tank destroyers can be seen in front. (US Army)**

E. M10 3-INCH GMC, 2E ESCADRON, 11E REGIMENT DE CHASSEURS D'AFRIQUE, ALSACE, MAY 1945

The French First Army, which served as part of the US Sixth Army Group, followed a standardized pattern of armored vehicle markings. The most distinctive sign was the Napoleonic regimental flash on the hull side in the national colors that was carried on all armored vehicles. Each unit had its own colored tactical sign, in this case, on a green square. The D on the square identified tank destroyer regiments later in the war. The bar above the D with the two pips indicates the 2nd Squadron, while the three separate pips around the periphery of the insignia indicates the 3rd platoon, commanded by Lt. Blania. The other vehicles in this platoon were named Essling, Eylau, Rivoli, and Iena. The marking on the right side of the bow and stern, a yellow C with colored bars, is part of an Allied system of shipping codes to keep track of units and their equipment during transit and after landing. On the center of the front and rear of the vehicle is the standard French Army registration number painted on a black rectangle and preceded by a national tricolor.

F. M36 90MM GMC, REGIMENT BLINDE COLONIAL D'EXTREME ORIENT, TONKIN, INDOCHINA, 1953

The French Army received M36 tank destroyers through the US Military Aid Program after World War II. These were of the late type with the added roof armor, and the extended end connectors on the track. French vehicles retained the basic olive drab color, or were repainted in a French Army

ABOVE **A far more practical approach to the need for a 90mm tank destroyer was the T71 which mounted a more refined 90mm tank gun in a new turret with ammunition stowage in the rear bustle. In contrast with the production M36 90mm GMC, the pilots had a slight bulge in the left rear side of the turret to accommodate a ring mount as seen in this overhead view. (US Army)**

equivalent. The markings include the RBCEA insignia, a white knight's helmet on a naval anchor which symbolizes the unit's deployment in the overseas colonies. The vehicle name is painted in white on the turret side, and the usual French Army registration number is on the hull side. Vehicles stationed in Indochina had the registration number starting in IC.

G1. M36 90MM GMC, YUGOSLAV PEOPLE'S ARMY, BALKAN WARS, 1996

Yugoslavia received the M36 and M36B1 as MAP aid in the 1950s. They were eventually repainted in the standard Yugoslav People's Army scheme, which was a gray-green color, noticeably lighter than the Warsaw Pact dark green.

Tactical markings were very sparse, a four-digit number in white on the upper turret front. During the civil war in Yugoslavia in the 1990s, some local militias repainted their M36s in far more elaborate schemes, but this vehicle remained in the pre-war colors until it was finally abandoned.

G2. M36B2 90MM GMC, TURKISH ARMY, 1953

Turkey received a number of M36 tank destroyers in the early 1950s as a stop-gap until better medium tanks became available. The color scheme was simple consisting of the usual US olive drab, with the national flag insignia on the turret. The registration number, on a white rectangle, was applied on the turret sides, as well as on the center of the hull front and rear.

BELOW **The Yugoslav People's Army (JNA) received M36, and M36B1 tank destroyers from the United States in the 1950s. These saw extensive combat use in the Balkans wars of the 1990s on various sides of the conflict. To keep these vehicles running, many were rebuilt with Soviet V-55 diesel engines like this example, currently preserved at the Virginia Military Vehicle Museum. (Author)**

INDEX